A First Thesaurus

Ruth Thomson

Belitha Press

D0544156

First published in the UK in 2001 by
Belitha Press,
an imprint of Chrysalis Children's Books plc
64 Brewery Rd, London N7 9NT

This paperback edition first published in 2002.
© Belitha Press Ltd 2001
Text © Ruth Thomson 2001
Illustrations © Belitha Press 2001

ISBN 1 84138 248 5 (hardback)
ISBN 1 84138 274 4 (paperback)

10 9 8 7 6 5 4 3 2 1 (hardback)
10 9 8 7 6 5 4 3 2 1 (paperback)

British Library Cataloguing in Publication Data for this book
is available from the British Library.

Editors: Stephanie Turnbull, Mary-Jane Wilkins, Terri McCargar
Designers: Rachel Hamdi, Holly Mann
Illustrators: Patrice Aggs, Becky Blake, Louise Comfort,
Charlotte Hard, Brenda Haw, Jan McAfferty, Kevin McAleenan,
Holly Mann, Melanie Mansfield, Colin Payne, Lisa Smith,
Sara Walker, Gwyneth Williamson
Educational consultant: Pie Corbett,
    Poet and Consultant to the
    National Literacy Strategy

Printed in Taiwan

Contents

What is a thesaurus?

A thesaurus is a treasure chest of words. You can use it to find exactly the right words you want for writing stories, poems, letters or reports.

In this thesaurus, there is a selection of words listed in alphabetical order. These are called **keywords**. They are mainly words that people use too much, such as *nice*, *said* and *went*.

Under each keyword are words that mean something similar. These are words that you could use instead of the keyword.

How to use this thesaurus

Look at this sentence:

> The **bad** wizard threw **bad** eggs at the **bad** thief.

To make this sentence more interesting, you might choose other words.

★ Look up the **keyword** *bad*. It is at the top of the page.

★ Find the **heading** that describes the meaning you want.

★ Choose a word from the **list** and try it out.

You could change the words in the sentence like this:

> The **wicked** wizard threw **stinking** eggs at the **sneaky** thief.

keyword

heading

list

bad

a bad person
evil
horrible
horrid
nasty
wicked

see also
nasty

opposite word
good

a bad animal
badly behaved
cheeky
mischievous
naughty

You **naughty** puppies!

bad behaviour
criminal
rotten
sneaky
villainous
wicked

feeling bad
ill
poorly
sick
unwell

food that has gone bad
mouldy
stale
sour
rotten
stinking

opposite word
fresh

bad weather see nasty

16 **a bad mood** see angry and sad

Opposite words are also given.

If you don't find the word you want, look up other **keywords** in the blue boxes.

Other ways to use this thesaurus

Sometimes each alternative word to the keyword has only one meaning. The pictures illustrate these meanings, to help you choose the word you need.

keyword

words for what someone ate **with**

words for different types of **meals**

words for different ways of eating

phrases for how people eat

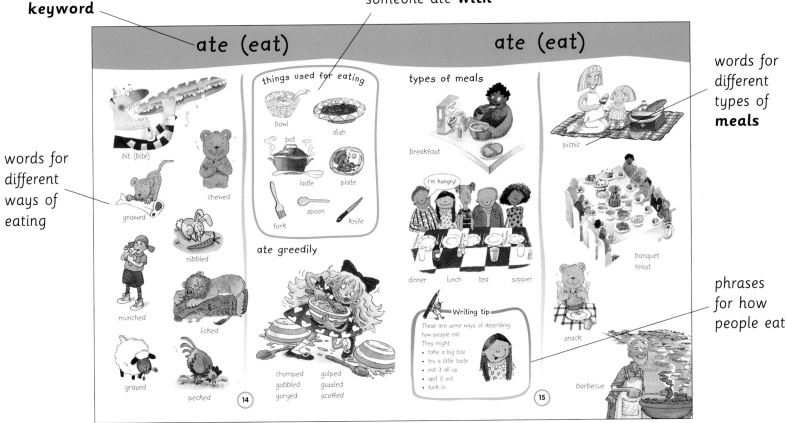

ate (eat)

things used for eating
bowl
dish
pot
ladle   plate
fork   spoon   knife

bit (bite)
chewed
gnawed
nibbled
munched
licked
grazed
pecked

ate greedily
chomped   gulped
gobbled   guzzled
gorged   scoffed

14

ate (eat)

types of meals
breakfast

I'm hungry!
dinner   lunch   tea   supper

Writing tip
These are some ways of describing how people eat. They might:
• take a big bite.
• try a little taste.
• eat it all up.
• spit it out.
• tuck in.

picnic

banquet feast

snack

barbecue

15

Look at this sentence:

Goldilocks **ate** some porridge.

It might be better to say how, when and with what Goldilocks ate the porridge.

⭐ Find the **keyword** ate.

⭐ Think about **how** Goldilocks ate.

⭐ What did she eat **with**?

⭐ Decide which **meal** Goldilocks ate.

A new sentence could be:

Goldilocks **guzzled** three **bowls** of porridge for **breakfast**.

Using the index

If the word you want to change is not a keyword, look it up in the **index** at the end of the book.

Nouns

Nouns are naming words for people, animals, things and places.

On these pages are three noun banks. Use them to help you choose people, things and settings for your stories.

Use the noun banks to make different, more exciting sentences.

For example, this sentence:

> The **boy** took a **box** to the **house**.

could be changed to:

> The **soldier** took a **map** to the **jungle**.
> The **princess** took a **ladder** to the **cliffs**.

People

alien

diver

King

knight

wizard

fairy

clown

inventor

prince

mermaid

soldier

magician

princess

queen

pirate

sailor

Things

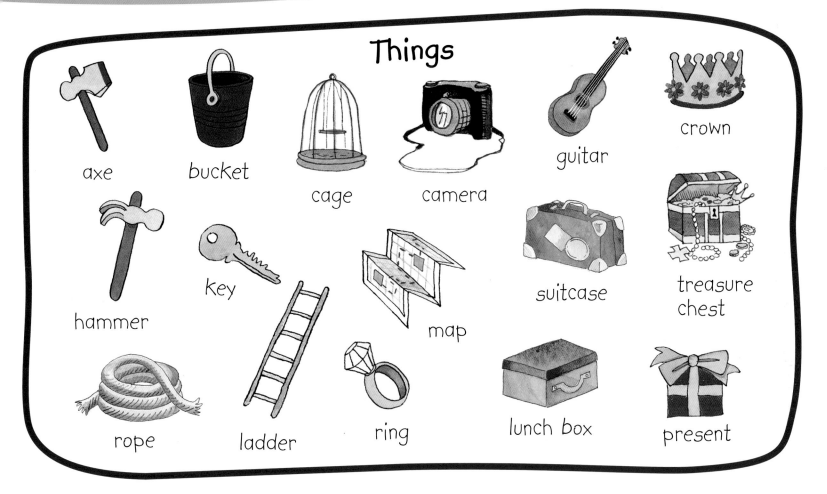

axe

bucket

cage

camera

guitar

crown

hammer

key

map

suitcase

treasure chest

rope

ladder

ring

lunch box

present

Settings

cliffs

desert

mountains

garden

island

woods

swamp

river

town

swimming pool

hill

jungle

Adjectives

Adjectives tell you more about nouns.

The two sentences below have no adjectives.

> Yesterday I met a wolf with eyes and eyebrows. I stared at his teeth and lips.

You can describe the wolf in more detail by adding adjectives, for example:

> Yesterday I met a **delightful** wolf with **enormous** eyes and **huge** eyebrows. I stared at his **golden** teeth and **rubbery** lips.

Can you write a description of a **scary** wolf, using different adjectives?

Use the thesaurus to help you. Look up the words in bold to choose suitable adjectives:

★ Are his eyes and ears **big** or **little**?

★ Is he **beautiful** or **ugly**?

★ Is he **nice** or **nasty**?

★ Is he **happy** or **angry**?

Colours are adjectives. Use extra words to describe a colour more exactly.

What is the colour of this crocodile?

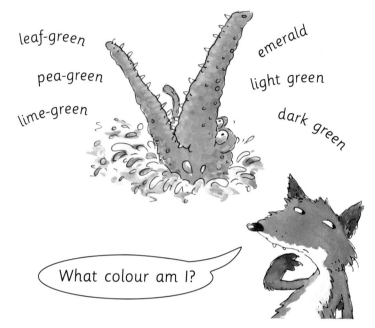

leaf-green
pea-green
lime-green
emerald
light green
dark green

What colour am I?

You can use adjectives to compare two things. Compare this monster with a snake. Choose adjectives from the box below to describe the differences between them.

shape: round thin fat long
size: tall tiny huge small colossal
colour: yellow green red blue black
way of moving: wriggly jumpy bouncy
weight: heavy light
texture: slimy furry scaly smooth
character: friendly fierce sly gentle

Verbs

Verbs are doing words. They tell you what is happening in a sentence. Compare the three sentences below.

The man **raked** the grass.

The man **dug up** the grass.

The man **mowed** the grass.

Each verb tells you exactly what the man did to the grass.

Look at the sentence below.

The crocodile **went** over the rock.

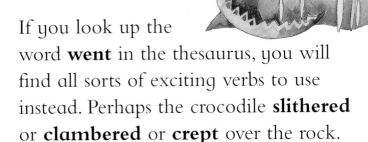

If you look up the word **went** in the thesaurus, you will find all sorts of exciting verbs to use instead. Perhaps the crocodile **slithered** or **clambered** or **crept** over the rock.

Now look up the verbs in the sentences below. Choose a more powerful verb.

The explorers **walked** through the jungle.

"Someone has stolen my jewels," **said** the queen.

Tenses

Verbs change to tell you whether an event is in the **past**, **present** or **future**. These are called tenses.

The verb in the sentence below tells you about something that has already happened, in the **past**.

When I **was** little, I **went** to nursery.

This sentence tells you what is happening now, in the **present**.

Now I **am** bigger, I **go** to primary school.

This one tells you about something that hasn't happened yet, but will happen in the **future**.

Later I **will go** to secondary school.

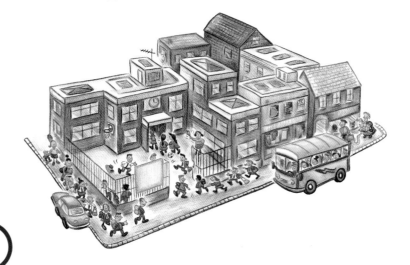

Most of the verbs in this thesaurus are in the **past** tense.

Joining words and punctuation

Joining words

You can make sentences longer and more interesting by using a **joining word** called a connective.

You can put one in the middle of a sentence to join two ideas.

The bees buzzed angrily around Mr Fox **when** he tried to steal their honey.

You can also use a joining word to link two sentences together.

I got a new bike today. **After** school, I tried it out in the park.

Joining words

and	after	so	then
while	because	next	until
but	or	first	when
finally	after that	if	before

Capital letters and full stops

Use a capital letter to begin every sentence, and put a full stop at the end.

One day, Mr Fox went rowing in a leaky boat. The boat began to sink.

Commas

When you write a long list, use commas to separate the things in the list.

In the canoe there were two sleeping bags, a torch, two paddles, a knife and a fishing rod.

If you use more than one adjective to describe something, separate the adjectives with a comma.

The knife was long, heavy and sharp.

Do not put a comma before the word **and**.

Speech marks

When you write down what people say, put **speech marks** at the beginning and end of the words they speak.

⭐ Start on a new line when a new person speaks.

⭐ Put the punctuation inside the speech marks.

"I don't know what to choose," Jo said.
Jon suggested, "Try the knickerbocker glory."

Question marks

If someone asks a question, put a **question mark** at the end of their words. Put the question mark inside the speech marks.

"Can you see that aeroplane?" asked the pilot.

"What kind is it?" inquired the woman.

"Where is it going?" asked the man.

Exclamation marks

If someone says something angrily or excitedly, or gives a command or a warning, put an **exclamation mark** at the end of their words.

"Come back!" cried the fan.

"Wait for me!" yelled the man.

"Help!" shouted the woman.

Exciting writing

Using this thesaurus, you can make your writing more powerful.

★ Write your first draft.

★ Read your draft. See if you can make it more exciting by choosing different words from this thesaurus and adding other details.

Sam went down the street to the sweet shop. He looked in the shop window. It was full of nice sweets.

He went inside and took some sweets.

The nice shopkeeper said, "Don't eat them all at once!"

cycled
Sam ~~went~~ down the street to ~~the~~   Mr Fudge's

gazed into
sweet shop. He ~~looked in~~ the shop

crammed with mouth-watering
window. It was ~~full of nice~~ sweets.

strolled in   chose some sticky toffees
He ~~went inside~~ and ~~took some sweets~~.

friendly   chuckled
The ~~nice~~ shopkeeper ~~said~~, "Don't   scoff
~~eat~~

them all at once!"

★ Write your final draft with all the new words.

Sam cycled down the street to Mr Fudge's sweet shop. He gazed into the shop window. It was crammed with mouth-watering sweets. He strolled in and chose some sticky toffees. The friendly shopkeeper chuckled, "Don't scoff them all at once!"

angry

bad-tempered
crabby
grouchy
grumpy
snappy

Writing tip

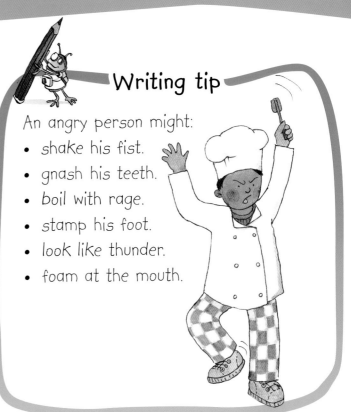

An angry person might:
- shake his fist.
- gnash his teeth.
- boil with rage.
- stamp his foot.
- look like thunder.
- foam at the mouth.

I'm **fed up**!

fed up   upset

very angry

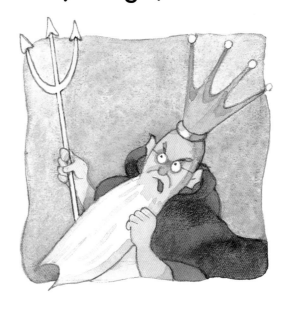

fuming
furious
livid
mad

annoyed
cross
irritated

Neptune was **furious** when divers found his underwater kingdom.

opposite words

happy
pleased

13

ate (eat)

bit (bite)

gnawed

chewed

nibbled

munched

licked

grazed

pecked

14

things used for eating

bowl

dish

pot

ladle

plate

fork

spoon

knife

ate greedily

chomped   gulped

gobbled   guzzled

gorged   scoffed

ate (eat)

types of meals

breakfast

I'm hungry!

dinner   lunch   tea   supper

picnic

banquet
feast

snack

barbecue

 Writing tip

These are some ways of describing how people eat.
They might:
- take a big bite.
- try a little taste.
- eat it all up.
- spit it out.
- tuck in.

bad

a bad person

evil
horrible
horrid
nasty
wicked

see also
nasty

opposite word

good

a bad animal

badly-behaved
cheeky
mischievous
naughty

You **naughty** puppies!

bad behaviour

criminal
rotten
sneaky
villainous
wicked

feeling bad

ill
poorly
sick
unwell

food that has gone bad

mouldy
stale

sour

rotten
stinking

opposite word

fresh

bad weather

see
nasty

a bad mood

see
angry and sad

beautiful

a beautiful person

elegant   smart
glamorous   well-dressed

attractive
charming
graceful
lovely
pretty

delightful
good-looking
gorgeous
handsome

opposite words

gruesome
hideous
horrible
ugly

a beautiful building

dazzling
grand
magnificent
splendid

a beautiful view

see
nice (view)

Writing tip

Read this story opening to see how you might change **beautiful** to some other words.

   charming   magnificent
A ~~beautiful~~ princess lived in a ~~beautiful~~

                handsome
castle with her ~~beautiful~~ brother.

           graceful
One day, a ~~beautiful~~

fairy appeared ...

big

a big person

enormous	hulking
hefty	large
huge	tall

a big animal

colossal
enormous
gigantic
huge
massive

a big mountain

enormous
high
huge
mighty
towering

a big river

long
wide

a big area

enormous
huge
immense
large
vast

big

a big hole

deep
huge
wide

a big building

colossal
enormous
immense
massive
roomy

high
tall

a big bang

deafening
ear-splitting
loud
mighty
noisy
tremendous

That was a **deafening** bang!

see also
noises

a big event

grand
important
impressive
spectacular
splendid

opposite words

little
small

Writing tip

Compare the size of something with
another thing. This gives readers
a better idea of how
big it is. This big
monster might be:

- as **huge** as
  a house.
- **bigger** than
  an elephant.

piece
portion
slab
slice
wedge

scrap
shred

chunk
hunk
lump
morsel
piece

dollop
forkful
mouthful
spoonful
taste

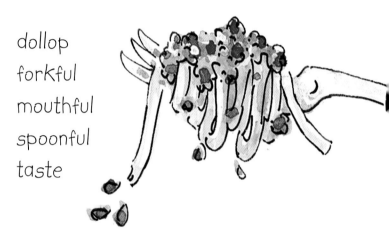

I've lost a **piece** of my jigsaw.

part
piece

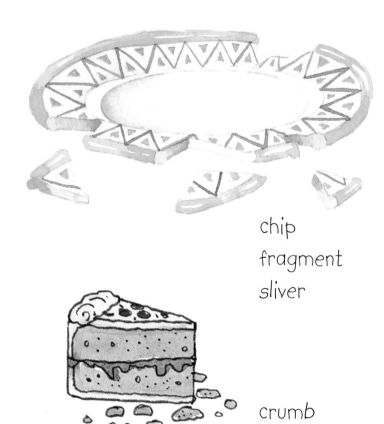

chip
fragment
sliver

crumb

bright

a bright object

dazzling
gleaming
glittering
shiny
sparkling

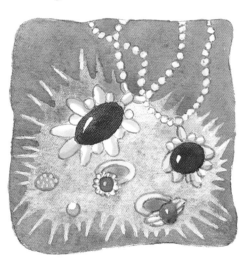

opposite words

dull   rusty

a bright light

blazing   gleaming
dazzling   glowing
glaring   twinkling

opposite words

dim   faint

a bright colour

brilliant
colourful
gaudy
vivid

a bright person or idea

brainy
brilliant
clever
intelligent
sharp
smart

opposite words

foolish   silly

a bright day
see
nice (weather)

bright (cheerful)
see
happy

cold

cold weather

chilly	icy
freezing	snowy
frosty	wintry

a cold wind

biting	icy
bitter	raw
chill	stinging

opposite word

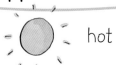 hot

feeling cold

freezing   frozen   shivery

opposite words

hot

warm

Writing tip

These are some different ways to describe how cold people are. They might:

- turn *blue* with cold.
- be *chilled to the bone.*
- have *teeth chattering* with cold.
- be *frozen stiff.*
- be *numb* with cold.
- have *feet like ice blocks.*

cried (cry)

bawled
wailed

blubbered
sniffed
snivelled
whimpered

sobbed
wept (weep)

howled
yowled

opposite word

laughed

---

cried out

called   shrieked
shouted   yelled

see also
said

Help!

"Help!" **shouted** the princess.

Writing tip

Use other ways to describe
how someone cries out.
They might:
- cry with delight.
- cry for help.
- cry for joy.
- cry with rage.
- cry in despair.
- cry with surprise.

dirty

filthy
greasy
grubby
stained
streaked

mucky
muddy

messy
untidy

opposite word

clean

foul
polluted
smoky

dusty
filthy
grimy

see also
nasty

drank (drink)

drank a little

sipped
tasted

drank greedily

gulped
guzzled
slurped
swigged

You drink from . . .

a beaker

a mug

a cup

a glass

a goblet

a bottle

cold drinks

water

juice
squash

fizzy drink

milk shake

hot drinks

coffee

tea

hot chocolate

frightened

afraid
fearful
scared
terrified

alarmed
shocked
startled

anxious
dismayed

nervous
worried.

opposite words

bold
brave
daring
fearless

opposite word

calm

astonished
startled
surprised

Writing tip

Someone who is very frightened might be:

• scared stiff.
• petrified.
• scared to death.
• panic-stricken.
• numb with fear.

full

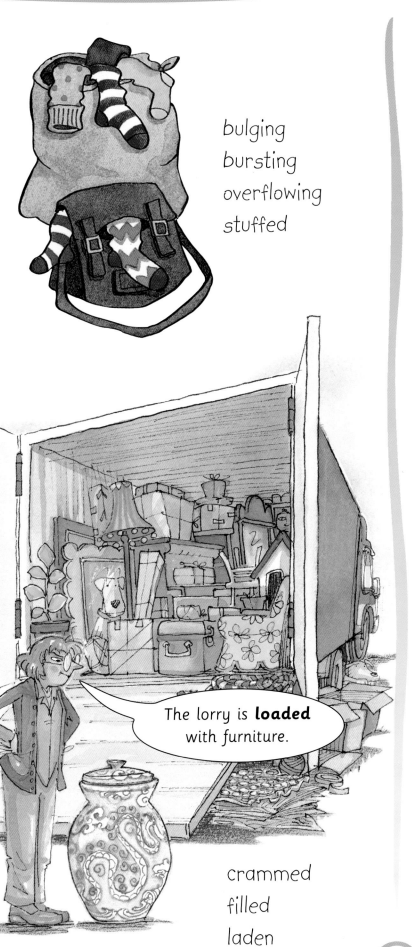

bulging
bursting
overflowing
stuffed

crowded
jammed
packed

This bus is very **crowded**.

The lorry is **loaded** with furniture.

crammed
filled
laden
loaded

brimming
heaped
overflowing
piled

opposite word

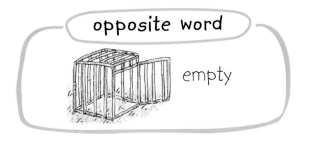

empty

good

a good film or book

That was an **exciting** film!

amazing
exciting
fantastic

gripping
incredible
thrilling

Writing tip

If you want to describe something good, you could say it is:

- action-packed.
- breathtaking.
- fast-moving.
- hair-raising.
- heart-stopping.
- spine-tingling.

a good mood

see
happy

good at something

experienced
expert
skilful
skilled
talented

a good time

We're having a **great** time!

brilliant
enjoyable
fabulous

great
terrific
wonderful

good

good behaviour

angelic
as good as gold
helpful
polite
well-behaved

opposite word

bad

good weather

see
hot and nice

a good idea

see
bright (person or idea)

good work

excellent
marvellous
perfect
splendid
superb

You have done **excellent** work!

a good person

You are very **kind**.

caring   helpful
friendly   Kind
                thoughtful

Writing tip

The sentences below show how you could use other words to replace good.

Yesterday we had a ~~good~~ *wonderful* day

out. We went to a ~~good~~ *thrilling* race.

Jimmy Beals, a really ~~good~~ *skilled*

driver, won first prize.

got (get)

got something from somewhere

collected
gathered
picked up

brought (bring)
fetched

got something from someone

received

was given

got a prize

gained
won (win)

I've **won** first prize!

got something from a shop

bought   chose   purchased
(buy)   (choose)

30

got (get)

got to a place
arrived   came (come)   reached

got hold of
caught (catch)
grabbed

got away
escaped
fled (flee)

got (became)

became (become)
grew (grow)
turned

The plant **grew** taller and taller.

The sky **turned** dark and stormy.

got a cold
caught (catch)

I think I've **caught** a cold.

31

happy

a happy person

bright
cheerful
jolly
joyful
merry

opposite word

sad

a very happy person

excited   gleeful   overjoyed   thrilled

happy about something

contented   delighted   glad   pleased

banged
bashed
battered
beat
hammered
thumped

hit with your fist

bashed
punched
smashed
swiped
thumped

hit with a bat

knocked
smacked
struck (strike)
swiped
walloped
whacked

ways a car hit something

banged into   crashed into
bumped into   rammed
collided with   smashed into

hit with a stick or finger

jabbed
poked
prodded
tapped

hot

hot weather

baking
blazing
boiling
roasting
scorching
sunny
sweltering

see also
nice (weather)

opposite word

cold

hot food

piping hot
sizzling
steaming

opposite word

cold

hot water or soup

boiling
bubbling
piping hot
scalding

a hot fire

blazing
flaming
glowing
red-hot
roasting
warm

Writing tip

Here are some words you could use
to describe the sounds of a **hot** fire.

crackle   fizz
pop   roar   hiss   sigh
snap   splutter

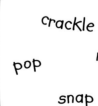

laughed (laugh)

smiled

beamed
grinned

chortled
chuckled
giggled
tittered

laughed loudly

cackled   howled
guffawed   roared

Writing tip

People who are laughing might:
- roar with laughter.
- split their sides laughing.
- fall about laughing.
- laugh their heads off.

laughed unkindly

jeered
made fun of
mocked
poked fun at
sneered
sniggered

opposite word

cried

little

a little person

short
slight
small
tiny

very little

minuscule
minute
teeny
tiny

a little space

narrow
tight

little (baby)

baby
wee
young

A kitten is a **young** cat.

There are special words
for many young animals.

cow   calf   duck   duckling

hen   chick   horse   foal

pig   piglet   sheep   lamb

bear   cub   Kangaroo joey

looked (look)

looked for a long time

gazed
glared
peered
stared

looked at secretly

peeked
peeped
spied

looked at quickly

glanced at
glimpsed
peeped at

looked at closely

observed
watched

examined
inspected

peered at
studied

looked for

hunted
looked high and low
nosed about

scouted around
searched

a lot of (things)

a collection
a jumble
a selection

a line of socks
a row

a heap
a pile
a stack

a mound of clay
a lump

a tower of bricks

a bunch of grapes

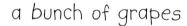

a hoard of treasure

a bunch of flowers

a bundle of sticks

a stack of plates

a string
of sausages

a garland
of flowers

a set of crockery

a chain of mountains
a range

a clump of trees
a forest
a wood

a lot of (people)

a queue

an army   a troop of soldiers

a band
a group of musicians

a crew of sailors

a gang
of pirates

a cluster
a crowd
a group
a horde

a lot of (animals)

a flock of sheep

a flock of birds

a herd of goats

a swarm of bees

an army of ants
a colony

a litter of puppies

a gaggle of geese

a school of whales

a pack of wolves

a shoal of fish

40

a pride of lions

nasty

a nasty person

cruel
horrible
mean
spiteful
unfriendly
unkind

opposite words

good   nice

a nasty smell

What's that **revolting** smell?

awful
revolting
rotten
sickening
stinking
vile

a nasty taste

disgusting
foul
revolting

see also
bad (food)

nasty weather

see also
cold (weather)
wet (weather)

dreadful   rainy
foul   rough
horrible   stormy
miserable   unpleasant

Writing tip

When you write about nasty weather,
use all your senses to describe it.
• What can you **see** - dark clouds, an
inky sky or bright flashes of lightning?
• What can you **hear** - wind moaning
and howling, thunder booming or
crackling?
• What can you **feel** - biting gusts
of wind or fat raindrops on your face?

nice

a nice person

charming   kind
generous   sweet
helpful   thoughtful

a nice-looking person

see
beautiful (person)

a nice view

amazing   enchanting   spectacular
beautiful   incredible   stunning

a nice time

brilliant
delightful
enjoyable
fantastic
great
wonderful

nice weather

bright
dry
fine
gorgeous
mild
pleasant
sunny
warm

opposite words

dull   cloudy
cool   grey
overcast

nice

This pudding is **yummy**!

nice food

delicious
mouth-watering
scrumptious
tasty
yummy

opposite words

disgusting
nasty
revolting

Writing tip

Use some of these words to describe the way different foods taste and feel – not all of them are nice!

spaghetti

hot
mushy
peppery
slimy
sloppy
squidgy

soup

chunky
creamy
fiery
hot
lumpy
peppery
salty
sloppy

fruit

crisp
crunchy
juicy
sour
sweet
tangy
tart

cake

crumbly
dry
gooey
light
spongy
squashy
stale
sticky
sugary
sweet

meat

crisp
greasy
hot
juicy
leathery
lumpy
rubbery
stringy
tender
tough

vegetables

crisp
crunchy
fresh
limp
salty
soggy
squashy
stringy

sweets

buttery
chewy
creamy
crunchy
minty
sticky
sugary

yogurt

creamy
fruity
smooth
tangy
thick

chillies

fiery
hot
spicy

noises

noisy

blaring
booming
loud
noisy
shrill

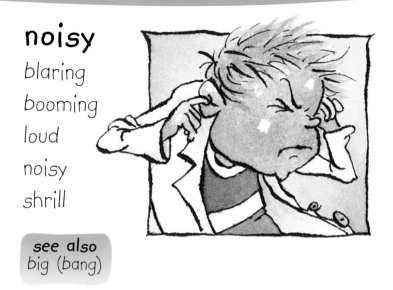

see also
big (bang)

opposite word

quiet

spooky noises

bang
bump
clank
clatter
creak
groan
clink
jangle
knock
howl
moan
rustle
rattle
screech
thud
shriek
thump
wail
whisper

noises people make

clap

snore

sniff
snivel

sing

blow a
raspberry

whistle

pant
puff
sigh

groan
wheeze

see also
cried
laughed
said

44

noises

machine noises

whine

whistle

whizz
tick

whirr

boom

splutter

chop

bang

fizz

click

bong

clatter

boing

chug

clink
drone
hum

clack
clunk

swish

rattle
twang

fire noises
see
hot (fire)

traffic noises
see
went (on wheels)

water noises
see
wet

wind noises

howl   shriek

moan   wail

roar   whistle

noises

animal noises

buzz hum

squeak squeal

hiss rattle

croak

yap whine yelp

snarl growl howl bark

roar bellow

moo low

miaow purr yowl hiss

neigh whinny

thunder trumpet

squeal snort snuffle

chatter jabber screech

snap roar growl snarl

bird noises

cheep sing chirp tweet warble twitter

screech

cluck cackle

gobble

honk hiss

quack

cock-a-doodle-doo

cheep peep

hoot

screech squawk

ran (run)

dashed
hurried
rushed
scrambled
sped
(speed)

jogged
raced
sprinted

see also
walked
went

ran after   ran away

chased
followed
raced after
rushed after

bolted
escaped
fled (flee)

ways animals run

A rabbit **hops**, **scurries** and **scampers** about.

A horse **trots**.

When horses run together in a panic, they **stampede**.

Crabs and spiders **scuttle**.

see also
went (animals)

When a horse runs fast, it **gallops**.

Writing tip

Words that describe the way animals run may also help you describe how a person moves, for example:

Class 2b **stampeded** out of school.
Tom **trotted** happily home.

sad

feeling sad

gloomy
glum
long-faced
miserable
troubled
unhappy

opposite word

happy

distressed
tearful
upset

sad news

dreadful terrible

grave tragic

serious upsetting

a sad story or show

Oh, what a **tragic** ending.

heart-breaking touching

moving tragic

tear-jerking unhappy

said (say)

see also
laughed
noises

That dog has ruined my shoes!

complained
groaned
grumbled
moaned

I'll buy you an ice-cream when we go out.

offered
promised

When water freezes, it turns into ice.

explained

I want my mummy!

sobbed
wailed
whimpered

see also
cried

I'm bored!

whined

Writing tip

When you write what someone said, put speech marks at the beginning and end of their words.

"I want my mummy!" **wailed** Tommy.

said (say)

argued   disagreed   insisted

asked   answered
replied

suggested   agreed

asked
begged
pleaded

ordered
warned

said (say)

said loudly

Look out!
Come back!

howled   shouted
screamed   shrieked
screeched   yelled

Ouch!

cried (out)
exclaimed
gasped
squealed

This bag is
so heavy.

said quietly

mumbled
murmured
muttered
sighed

hissed
whispered

said quickly

babbled   jabbered
gabbled   prattled

TheAfricanelephanthasbigearsandtusks.

said angrily

bellowed
demanded
roared
snapped
snarled
thundered

I want my
dinner NOW!

chucked
lobbed
tossed

scattered
sowed
spread
sprinkled

opposite word

caught
(catch)

threw hard

flung
(fling)

hurled

slung
(sling)

juggled

hurled   pelted   showered

took (take)

made off with
pinched
stole (steal)

captured
caught (catch)
kidnapped
seized

grabbed
seized
snatched

Give it back!

clasped
clutched
grasped
gripped
held (hold)

brought (bring)
carried
delivered
transported

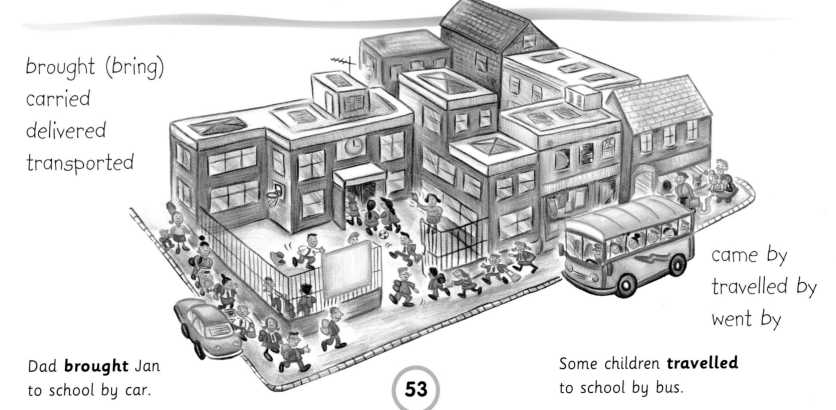

came by
travelled by
went by

Dad **brought** Jan
to school by car.

Some children **travelled**
to school by bus.

walked (walk)

walked a long way

hiked
rambled
tramped
trekked
trudged

walked quietly

crept (creep)
tiptoed

walked with difficulty

hobbled
limped
shuffled
staggered
stumbled
tottered

went for a gentle walk

ambled   sauntered   wandered
dawdled   strolled

walked with long steps

marched
strode (stride)

walked on something

stepped on   trod (tread)
trampled

*Jim's dog **trampled** on the flowers.*

went (go)

went on land

see also
ran
walked

jumped
leapt (leap)

danced
twirled

skated

climbed

crawled

hopped
skipped

skied

slid (slide)
whizzed
zipped
zoomed

spun (spin)
turned
twirled
whirled

55

went (go)

went on wheels

cycled
pedalled
rode (ride)

scooted

whizzed

drove (drive)   raced along
left (leave)   sped (speed)
set off   zoomed

Writing tip

To make your writing more powerful, write about car noises and traffic sounds.

drone

clatter

beep   chug

honk

screech   roar purr

hum   toot   wail

wheeled transport

bike

jeep

bus

scooter

car

tractor

cart

train

coach
(and horses)

tricycle

56

went (go)

went in water

dived
plunged

swam (swim)

dabbled
paddled

splashed
waded

drifted
floated
rowed

sailed

surfed

capsized
sank (sink)
went down

water transport

barge

submarine

canoe

tanker

hovercraft

trawler

liner

tug

speedboat

yacht

went (go)

went in the air

darted
flew (fly)
flitted
fluttered

blasted off
rose (rise) into the air
soared
took off (take off)

drifted
fell (fall)
floated
glided
wafted

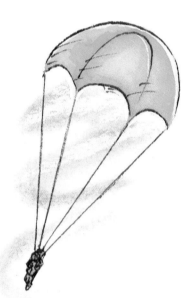

hovered

flashed
flew (fly)
hurtled
sped (speed)
streaked
tore (tear)
zoomed

air transport

aeroplane

jet

biplane

parachute

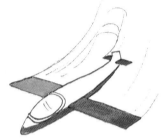

glider

rocket

helicopter

hot-air
balloon

spaceship
UFO

58

went (animals)

swung
(swing)

slid (slide)
slithered
squirmed
wiggled
wriggled

clambered
crawled
crept (creep)
crouched

flapped
glided
hovered
soared
swooped

darted
glided
swam (swim)
wiggled

bobbed
frisked
gambolled
leapt (leap)
pranced
skipped

see also
ran (animals)

danced
darted
flapped
flew (fly)
flitted
fluttered

prowled
stalked

bounced   jumped
bounded   leapt (leap)
hopped   sprang (spring)

Writing tip

Words that tell you how animals move may also help you describe how a person moved, for example:

Asha **slithered** behind the bush, out of sight.

Sara **fluttered** with excitement.

59

wet

wet weather

drizzly
pouring
rainy
showery
spitting

clammy   misty
damp   moist
humid   sticky

wet ground

boggy   spongy
marshy   squelchy
soggy   swampy

wet clothes

drenched
dripping
soaking
sopping
wringing wet

opposite word

dry

Writing tip

Use some of these words
for watery noises.   drip drop

splish splash splosh   sputter

burble gurgle   murmur   swish

pitter patter

plip plap plop

60

Index